DECEIVED BY EVIL

A GREAT SACRIFICE

John Daniel Roberts

NOT FOR CHILDREN,
PARENTAL CONSENT
ADVISED!

WRITERS REPUBLIC L.L.C.
515 Summit Ave. Unit R1
Union City, NJ 07087, USA

Website: *www.writersrepublic.com*
Hotline: *1-877-656-6838*
Email: *info@writersrepublic.com*

Ordering Information:
Quantity sales. Special discounts are available on quantity purchases by corporations, associations, and others. For details, contact the publisher at the address above.

Library of Congress Control Number: 2021923667
ISBN-13:   978-1-63728-995-2   [Paperback Edition]
            978-1-63728-996-9   [Digital Edition]

Rev. date: 11/19/2021

To the God who saved me and second, to the twin towers who strengthened me equally in the different places of my need. Women in whom my life was meant to increase with. An increase that only a Sovereign God could've orchestrated. These two women were paramount in the trajectory my life would take, in spite of my own selfish desire to do it my way. Yet "paramount" is an understatement in regards to how their love for me impacted my life.

Although my mom is not physically present with us, her love for me still keeps me steady. Even as the love from my wife of thirty-one years still inspires me to never give up. So too does her tenacity as a woman of God, continuously pushes towards hope. And just as my mom had been a place of retreat and solace in my life before my dear wife, I now find it even more so in Sheila. And, oh, how I thank God every day for my gift. Yet without question, these two ladies have been the instruments by which the hand of God has kept me. And so this book is indeed dedicated to the balance that both ladies have brought to my life. I thank God for allowing my wife and me to share our first seven years of marriage with my mom before her departure on New Year's Day, 1997. And I especially thank God for gracing me with my Sheila for the last twenty-four years since my mom's home going. Sheila has been my inspiration, the anchor God placed in my life to keep me grounded.

INTRODUCTION

A Paradoxical Dream
Eccl 11:10 / Dan 12:11/ Mt 24:15-16

It was early August 1991. I was out of work and had a lot of downtime. My wife was the only one employed, money was very tight, and we were barely making ends meet. And on this particular day, I had an early morning appointment at the Salvation Army (downtown Charleston, South Carolina) in hopes of receiving some rental assistance. But, of course, they were short on funds. After no success from that venture, I continued my job search efforts, to no immediate avail. Shortly after arriving home, and a cold glass of water, I decided to take a nap. I immediately began to dream. I was transported to a former time in my life. A time when it seemed as if I was going from one funeral to the next, either as a pallbearer or just there to witness another one of my friends being put in the ground. And not one of them dying because of sickness or disease, but some type of accident or violent death. And so here I was at another funeral, this time for a very close friend. His nickname was Cowboy. He'd died in a terrible car accident. And to me, his death was very significant. It was one of those "Hmm' moments that make you began to think seriously about growing up. But it hit me especially hard because earlier that evening, Cowboy and I shared a couple of drinks together as he prepared for a softball game, and as we shared those moments, I recalled six months earlier how I had disrespected him **in his new Cadillac** after a few too many drinks. And I asked him to forgive me for that episode so many months ago. I remember we laughed, and then his last words to me about it, was: "JD, we are friends, I'd forgotten all about that incident, but I'll say this—you and I will never have to worry about anything like that happening again. We are friends." Later that same night, he was killed in a freak car accident. Fast-forward to the funeral, I was one of the pallbearers and was very honored to be named among them. And after the funeral, I meandered around for a little while, offering my condolences to those that I'd not previously done so, before I finally managed to slip away. Now at this junction, my dream came back into focus, and still dreaming I headed home. And as soon as I was behind my doors, I headed straight for the shower, looking to wash the gloom away. After showering, I managed to eat a little bit; and after accomplishing that feat, I then headed for my couch, on the way picking up the newspaper. I slid lazily onto my couch.

Finally relaxed, I randomly opened my newspaper, and wouldn't you just know it, it fell open to the obituary section. And suddenly, in an instant, I was transported out of this dream into the dream for which this book is titled, *Deceived by Evil*!

So I believe that when you read this book, it will be one of the "Hmm' moments in your crossroad. Hence, I know you'll be enlightened. Now, I do believe God gave me this awesome book in the fullness of time, and for such a time as now so that as we grow up, we become the children of inheritance of our spiritual place in the Beloved. We will begin to rightly divide between good and evil as we come to the truth about what is passing away and how we're to live while passing through. And for me, it helped me to finally realize that we're not really in control of many aspects of our lives, where the intangibly invisible; intersect with the visible realities of life.

Hence, this fictional story that I dreamed, titled *Deceived by Evil*, I believe, was given to me as a warning, alerting those of us who will heed to the agenda of darkness that lurks not only outside of us, but especially inside of us. This story, I hope, will make us more aware of the ancient evil, which is that old serpent, Lucifer, whose many names are listed among all the people groups in the world. It has been here in its present form since its fall, and its purpose is to sift us in our weakness and to ultimately destroy us. And so I hope that in the pages of this book, the audience comes climatically to a place of recognition, recognizing that there is a devil and there is evil. But there is also an answer: Christ is His name, and He is good. And because of Him, we have the opportunity to grow up.

> *When I was a child, I spoke and thought and reasoned as a child.*
> *But when I grew up, I put away childish things.*
>
> —*1 Corinthians 13:11 (NLT)*

I saw a house from within. In it, there arose a great evil.

The evil manifested itself in the caricature of a friendly circus bear. The Evil One stood calm among the children while they played.

Their ages ranged from toddler to first grader. They were family and friends. But because of their innocence, they were ignorant to what they should fear since they'd not yet been properly introduced to evil. Hence, they did not yet know that the Bear was evil and that his intent was just that. But how could they know since they all saw him loving the children at the circus.

So the Horror stood smiling at the children, glowing in a color of deceit and dishonesty, basking in the true purpose for his presence with the children. And with a look of contentment, he engulfed himself in a mockery of love and respect for his unwitting prey—a respect for them in which he could never know.

And while Evil contemplated its next move, the children played. They played with a zest for life, the way children always play. They played as if there would be no tomorrow. And while they were embroiled in their fun and activities, Evil stood patiently calm, watching over them as though it were their hired nurse. Indeed, he watched with the patience of a hen brooding over her chicks.

Yet there was one of them who felt deception creeping over them like a dark shadow blocking out the sun. And though she was the youngest of them, she still felt the stirring of evil invading her soul, a slow creeping harshness that seemed to envelop her and her playmates. But because she was just a toddler, she'd not yet learned how to communicate in the verbiage of her peers.

She began to reason to herself (as a toddler reasons), and by her own deduction, she realized instinctively that she had to warn her playmates. And with great purpose, she began to crawl frantically around the room, from one friend to the other. But in all honesty, her frantic outburst in vying for her friend's attention was not so different from how she normally acted. After all, she was just a toddler, still a baby to her older playmates, though they themselves were also babes in the adult world. And so without any success in arousing her friends to the danger that loomed over them, they continued their fun and games.

But as she persisted in her effort to set off the alarm, which for the moment only she could hear, the atmosphere of fun that permeated their play was slowly and uncannily changing. And though they still could not hear the alarm that their little friend had sounded (since it seemed that she was the only one gifted with spiritual intuition), their natural senses were alerted. Yet now it was clear to the toddler, that despite all her effort of warning, she now knew that she was in the fight alone with the terror.

They had no clue of what real evil felt like, though they were taught in children's church that there is a devil and you will know him by his pitchfork, horns, and pointy tail. But their parents didn't tell them that Evil is a power of hell, and when left unchecked by parents and others who are not wise to it's devices and dark intentions then they unwittingly allow Evil to prey upon their children's innocence.

But thank God for the gift of discernment bestowed upon the toddler. Because of it, the spiritual eyes of her playmates were opened up to the horror standing in front of them, although they still yet have no clue as to the full impact of the Bear's deception on them and what it all meant. Nor did they fully understand how their toddler pal, the youngest of them all, had seen the danger before they did since they were older. But it was obvious to them now that she was special and that she had a gift of some sort and that they would one day thank her for it.

But now, because of the toddler's inexhaustible effort to alert her friends, the Bear began to sense the panicked-stricken energy of the toddler. But as horrid as Evil is, it still can't discern or read the minds of the children.

And so the Bear slowly became aware that his intentions were no longer secret. The toddler's warnings were successful, and the truth to the Bear's deception was out in the open. And so the Evil One began to move in slow deliberation in the direction of the toddler while her friends looked on in a hypnotic gaze of enchanted dismay as if they were in a fairy tale (playing with their favorite toy watching as it began to come alive). While their minds grasp to understand what was going on, their eyes began to witness the metamorphosis of the giant teddy as he began to show its true colors and the true purpose for his disguise. Now the children began to move in a slow motion stupor, becoming bluntly aware of the apparent danger that they were all in. Hell was about to wreak havoc, gripping them in its maze of deception, and there was no place to run.

The children were mesmerized by Evil as they stood **helplessly by,** while their friend began to crawl frantically around them, trying to evade the gaze of the deranged Bear. She was sensing in every fiber of her being the danger her life was in. And out of sheer desperation and life-preserving instinct, she skillfully scooted across the floor, crawling from room to room in a desperate attempt to make it to her bedroom as the Darkness chased her with the prowess and stealth of a determined stalker. With her every maneuver, the Bear was on her heels, no longer cloaked in the disguise of deception. He had to stop the toddler before the minds of her fear-shocked playmates awakened.

And as he was now in striking distance and ready to engage with ferocious impact, the toddler was intensely focused on making it to her bedroom, her place of safety. Deep in her soul and in her mind, she believed that somehow if she could just make it to her bed, she would be safe, like so many times before when she was harassed by the shadows in the dark. She would retreat beneath the comfort of her cover, finding her safe place, until the morning light would break through. Yet this time, even in her hope, she felt that this was different.

And, of course, even in her limited life experience, this was a different emotion, one she had never experienced before. But deep in her soul she knew she couldn't give up. So she fought from the very essence of her soul, not surrendering, but holding on to all she'd ever known. Yet inside, she felt the total exertion of her strength ebbing from her soul. And yes, she knew that all her effort would soon come for naught and, without a doubt, her short-lived life would soon come to a violent close. Yet knowing all that, her desire to live was still palpable. And with her last burst of life force, she propelled herself onto her bed, snatching the covering over her head with a confidence that only a child would have in the naivety of their innocence. Her bed was the only place of safety from the invisible bogeyman.

Evil strikes!

As Evil struck, her friends stood in complete and utter shock. For what seemed like an eternity, they were unable to move. Then suddenly, like a fast-forward video, they were jolted out of their state of stupor and back to the reality of the horror that gripped them. And right in the middle of their awakening, they were again frozen in sheer terror as Evil ripped the flesh off the backside of their friend. They watched as it tore into the flesh of the babe with devastating force as if to send a message to them of it's utter contempt for their existence and to obliterate the truth represented in the innocence of the child—an innocence that bore record to what it means to sacrifice for love. And in her sacrifice, the heart of God is revealed, which is only privy to humans.

With his razor teeth dripping with torn flesh and blood, the Evil One slowly moved in stealth precision toward the other children, aiming with intent the full force of its diabolical agenda upon them. *Still with a tantalizing look of deceit in its eyes,* he looked at them. But as he gazed, the children instantly grew up. They morphed right before the eyes of their enemy. With the weight of their friend's brutal death still thick in the atmosphere, they immediately felt the impact of her great sacrifice. And because of the mortifying pain of their present reality, they grew up.

And suddenly, just as the Bear had appeared, he vanished. The giant circus bear was gone, leaving behind the shattered lives of its prey. The damage was done. They looked at one another in complete despair at the thought of how badly they would miss their friend. Even as their mourning had not yet truly begun, they felt the impact of her invisible presence.

They stood exhausted from the ordeal, looking dumbfounded in each other's gaze. They ruminated, then simultaneously came to the reality that even with numbers, there is no safety. When naivety is your enemy, and innocence is not a virtue. But a room where secrets hurt you and where a lack of spiritual discernment will destroy you. And with this new view and reckoning of life, they are now spiritually aware of how deceptive the desolation of abomination moves into the familiar places of their vulnerability and how the agenda of its purpose is always hiding in plain sight. It is continuously striving and studying with great disdain how to pluck them out of their places of safety in this world, drooling with a voracious appetite over a chance to devour them all (us all) so as to simply annihilate any resemblance of their Creator.

Therefore remove sorrow from your heart, and put away evil from your flesh. For childhood and youth are fleeting.
—Eccl 11:10 / Dan 12:11/ Mt 24:15-16

Parents, please teach your children to know the truth before Evil strikes!

So when I had this dream, I immediately knew it was something I had to share. This book is the format and tool by which the Holy Spirit impressed upon me what I would expose my audience to. My hope is that you will walk away more sensitive to spiritual things, most of all to the Spirit of God who is already in us as our life force. Hence, this story is about a unique relationship between a toddler and her more mature playmates. A story of a toddler with the gift of discernment, and inexpressible care she had for her friends—inexpressible by word, yet powerfully expressed in her effort to save her friends from the sifting of the enemy. So my hope is that when you read this book, you will come away with a deep sense of community and with a deeper understanding of self-sacrifice as well as with a sharpened knowledge of the presence of evil working in and around us all, trying with great stealth to reduce us to the elements of our desires and base us to our wanton desires.

And if this book delivers anything of value to the reader, let it be at least an awareness of their own vulnerability to the childlike naivety that lie prominent, in some capacity, within their own life space and how so very easily evil can creep in unaware, working within the ignorance that lie inside us all to our detriment, thus the motive and purpose of this book and its title, Deceived by Evil. Therefore, in the pages of this book, I admonish you to listen for the Spirit of truth in your life and lean on It so that you may discern the evil agenda that your Bear, or any other Evil Entity, has in store for you and the people you love.

YES,
EVIL
IS REAL

EPILOGUE

Yes, Evil Is Real

In this dream, a living nightmare, the subject matter is very sensitive to me because it's about children, children that became the target of a sinister plot. Much like all the unseen plots that develop around us every day, these unseen plots are thwarted and never materializes into reality because of a merciful God, a God concerned for His creation. But because the world we all call home is of a fallen nature, even good little children fall prey to Evil and its evil contemporaries.

And of course, we cannot ever be naïve about evil, by defining evil in politically correct terminologies. There's no such invented words that can usurp the power or the dynamics of evil and its processes in its exploits of destruction. Yes, evil is real, just as all things created has an opposite power of unity or disunity. Hence, there is good and evil.

And whether we believe in either entity or not, it doesn't change the reality of my dream and this fictional story. The bear was evil, and the toddler is dead. But of course, to prove that evil is real, just look at the news. Read a newspaper or turn on any TV program and look at the made-up and the real mayhem that write the script for the horror film industry. And after you've absorbed it all, wake up and tell me was it all just a dream or just a figment of your imagination. Yet if you take a closer look at yourself in the mirror and be honest with yourself, you will not be able to deny that good and evil exist. Why? Because the mirror shows you both sides of the coin—the good and the evil.

Train up a child in the way he should go; even when he is old he will not depart from it.

FINAL WORD

And so, as you spiritually nurture and care for your children, not only must you instruct them in the reality of good and evil but also in the differences and the end results of the two. Teach them to listen and discern who and what evil is! Teach them that the author of evil is the devil. From the day he was kicked out of heaven until he entered the earth, evil was not found. Teach them that he is no respecter of age, race, gender, or anything that is called mankind. And the younger and more vulnerable they are, without your help, they will become kindling for his fire. Just look at the news from whatever medium you choose, and you will see a multiplicity of ways that our children are destroyed or killed. They are needlessly dying in many horrific ways, but why? How can they be so vulnerable? For me, the answer is simple. Because, many times, we as their parents are releasing them into the world, even as we were. Grown-up in appearance only but as unprepared as the children were in this book.

So the hope in this fictional story, which was born out of my own tragic experiences, is that parents would do better than my own God-fearing Christian parents and teach their children the spiritual truths about good and evil and begin to prepare them early about life and death and all the tangible good and evil deeds done between the lines of their living, so that they will grow up with a spiritual maturity and awareness of their vulnerabilities in a fallen world. A world that does not have God as its center, nor in its straight and narrow way. Hence, our children must be prepared to navigate the kingdom of God through a maze of darkness and all kinds of wicked manipulations in order to be fruitfully productive, sowing love and bringing personal joy to their own lives.

For His glory, Amen!

CPSIA information can be obtained
at www.ICGtesting.com
Printed in the USA
BVHW091545141221
624016BV00002B/60